The Great Barrier Reef

Cheryl Jakab

The Great Barrier Reef

Text: Cheryl Jakab
Editor: Rebecca Crisp
Design: Jennifer Warwick
Series design: James Lowe
Photo researcher: Lisa Piemonte
Production controllers: Renee Cusmano and Lisa Porter
Reprint: Jennifer Foo

Acknowledgements
The author and publisher would like to acknowledge permission to reproduce material from the following sources:
Commonwealth of Australia: p.18 (photograph courtesy of Great Barrier Reef Marine Park Authority for and on behalf of the Commonwealth of Australia); Corbis Australia: p. 16; © David Wachenfeld/AUSCAPE all rights reserved: pp. 14, 21; Getty Images: p. 7 (top), 13 (inset), 20; Georgette Douwma/Naturepl.com: p. 19; © John Easley Photography 2008: p. 12; Jurgen Freund/Naturepl.com: p. 11 (bottom), 15; Kelvin Aitken/ANTPhoto.com.au: p. 13 (main); Michael Pitts/Naturepl.com: p. 10 (top); Photolibrary: pp. 3, 4–5,
7 (bottom), 8, 10 (bottom), 11 (top), back cover; Richard Morden © Cengage Learning Australia: pp. 6, 17; Tourism Queensland: pp. 1, 9, 22–23, cover.

Every effort has been made to trace and acknowledge copyright. However, if any infringement has occurred, the publishers tender their apologies and invite the copyright holders to contact them.

Fast Forward Independent Texts
Level 17

ISBN 978 0 17 017984 3
ISBN 978 0 17 017898 3 (set)

Cengage Learning Australia
Level 7, 80 Dorcas Street
South Melbourne, Victoria Australia 3205
Phone: 1300 790 853

Cengage Learning New Zealand
Unit 4B Rosedale Office Park
331 Rosedale Road, Albany, North Shore NZ 0632
Phone: 0800 449 725

For learning solutions, visit **cengage.com.au**

Printed in Australia by Ligare Pty Ltd
4 5 6 7 8 9 10 22 21 20 19 18

The Great Barrier Reef

Cheryl Jakab

Contents

CHAPTER 1

The Greatest Reef

Australia is home to one of the world's natural wonders – the Great **Barrier** Reef.

Each year, many people come from all over the world to see the Great Barrier Reef.

In 1981, the whole reef was listed as a World Heritage Area.

About 1.6 million people visit the Great Barrier Reef Marine Park each year.

A World Heritage Area is a protected area that is culturally or naturally important.

The Great Barrier Reef runs along part of the east coast of Australia. It is more than 2000 kilometres long and it makes a natural barrier between the land and the sea.

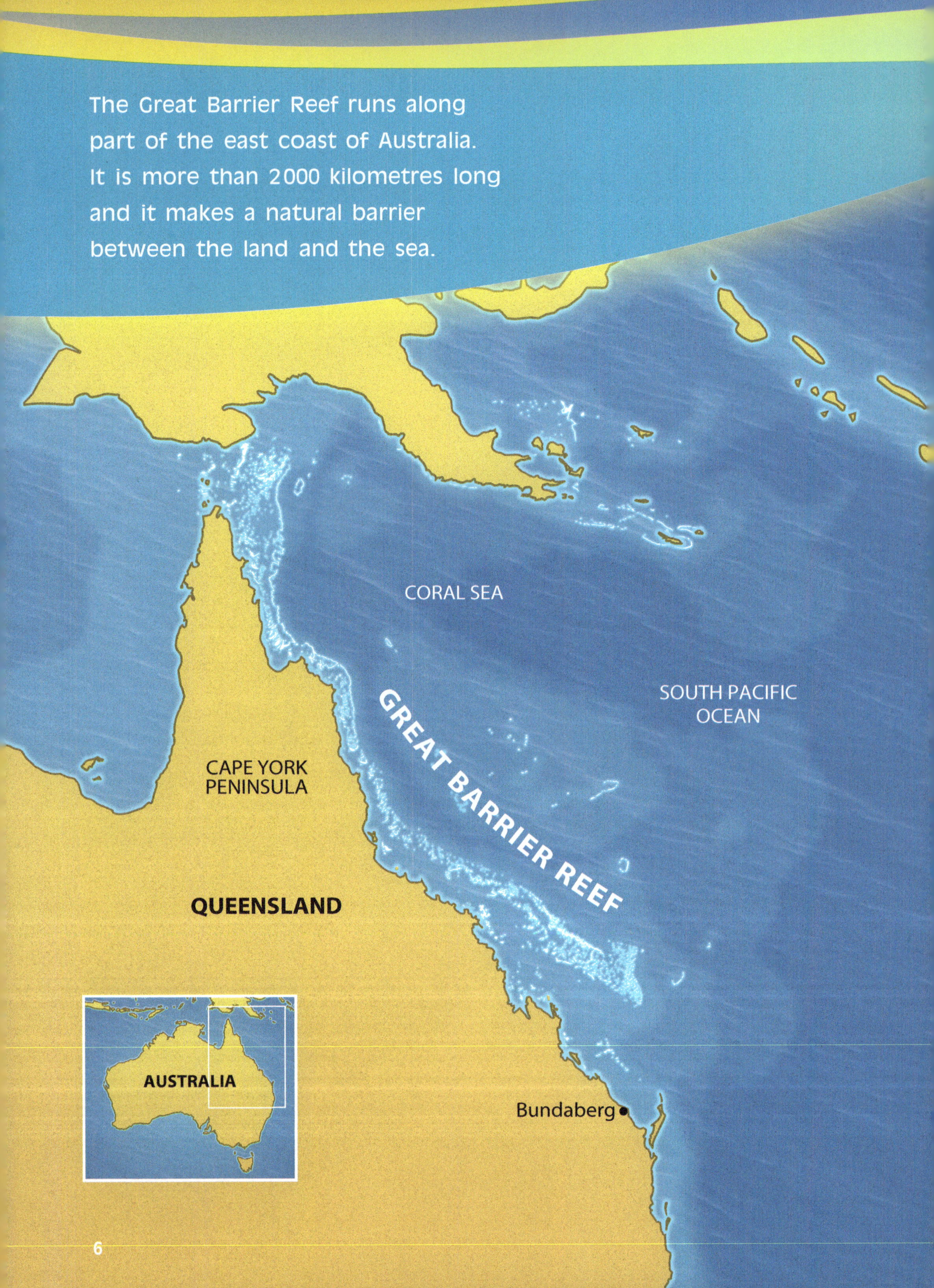

The Great Barrier Reef is the largest coral reef system in the world.
It covers an area larger than Italy.

It is made up of nearly 3000 individual coral reefs and over 600 islands.

Green Island is one of over 600 islands on the Great Barrier Reef.

The Great Barrier Reef has been growing for many thousands of years.
It is the world's biggest living structure and it is still growing today.

a satellite photo showing the Great Barrier Reef

The warm ocean waters off Australia's east coast are just right for **tropical** coral reefs. The water must be clear, not too salty and at least 18 °C all year round for tropical corals to grow.

CHAPTER 2

Corals of the Reef

There are about 400 types of corals on the Great Barrier Reef. Each type of coral grows in its own way and has its own shape, size and colour.

Some corals look like balls, and some look like trees. Others look like fans.

Corals can be pink, red, yellow, blue and many other colours.

Some kinds of corals can grow to up to 1.5 metres wide, high and long.

Coral Polyps

The Great Barrier Reef has been built up
by tiny animals called coral polyps.
Polyps live on top of the reef.
They have hard outer skeletons
and when they die,
their skeletons become part of the reef.

Each coral polyp can be from 3 to 56 millimetres wide or tall.

Some coral polyps of the Great Barrier Reef live in **partnership** with algae.

The algae give the corals most of their colours.

Without the algae, the corals would be white.

Coral Young

Some corals in the reef produce **young** by **splitting** to make new corals. This is called budding.

Other corals produce young by **spawning**. All the corals spawn at once. Spawning occurs in October each year, usually around a full moon.

corals spawning

CHAPTER 3

Life on the Reef

The Great Barrier Reef is like a city under the sea. Thousands of different ocean plants and animals live there.

Great Barrier Reef Animals

- 1 500 types of fish
- 400 types of coral
- 4000 types of mollusc
- 215 types of bird
- 16 types of sea snake
- 6 types of sea turtle

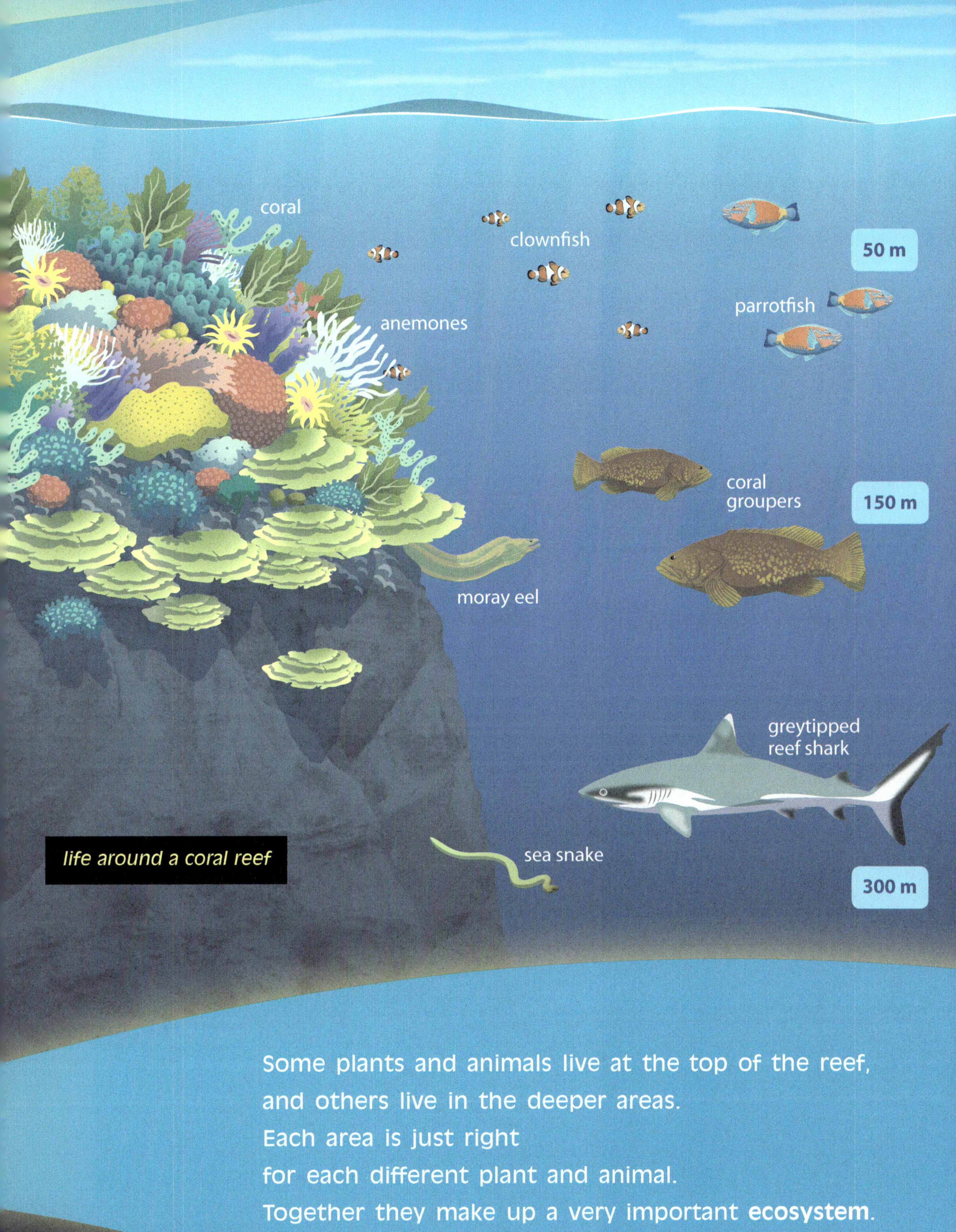

Some plants and animals live at the top of the reef,
and others live in the deeper areas.
Each area is just right
for each different plant and animal.
Together they make up a very important **ecosystem**.

CHAPTER 4

Dangers to the Reef

The Great Barrier Reef has been protected as a marine park since 1975.

marine park rangers

But there are still some big dangers to the reef and to everything that lives around it.

a crown-of-thorns starfish

The Crown-of-Thorns Starfish

The crown-of-thorns starfish is a danger to the reef because it feeds on coral polyps.
There are so many crown-of-thorns starfish that they are killing areas of the reef.

Pollution

Another danger to the reef is pollution.

Many tourists visit the reef each year and the boats that carry the tourists pollute the water around the reef with **fuel**.

Tourism brings a lot of money to the reef, but it also hurts the reef.

Climate Change

The greatest danger to
the Great Barrier Reef is climate change.
Climate change is making the sea warmer,
and this can kill the corals.
The reef can only live
if the sea stays the right temperature.

This coral has died because the sea temperature is too high.

CHAPTER 5

Protecting the Reef

The Great Barrier Reef is a very important ecosystem. It is the biggest and healthiest tropical reef system on Earth. But everyone must do their part to help protect it.

The Marine Park Authority is working with the Australian Government to stop the dangers to the reef, so that it can live long into the future.

Glossary

barrier something that prevents movement

ecosystem a community of living and non-living things

fuel a substance that powers a machine

partnership an arrangement whereby two living things provide support to one another

spawning the release of eggs and sperm into the water

splitting dividing into two or more pieces

tropical in a warm place on Earth

young babies; offspring

Index